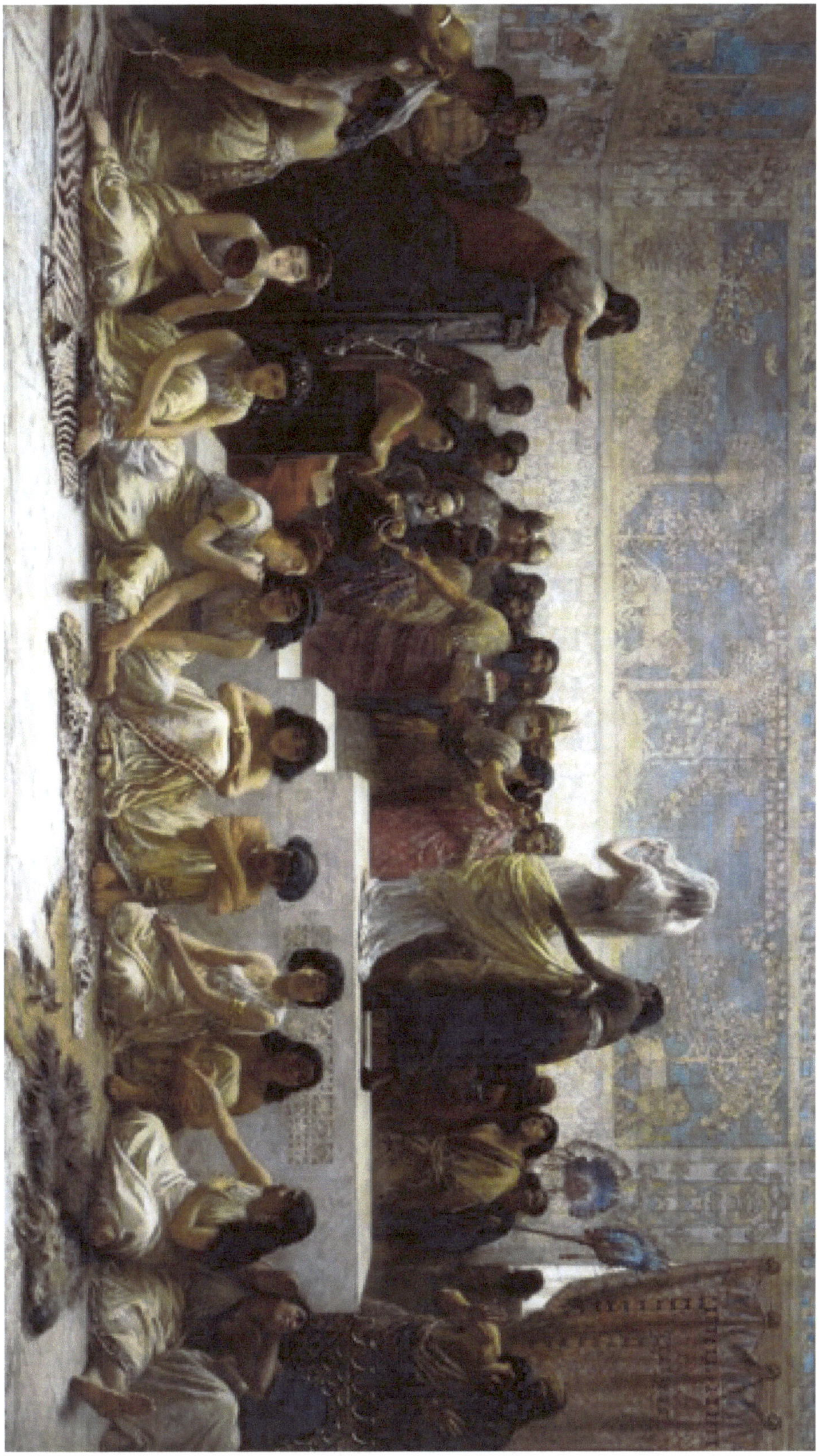

Slavery in Art   Edited by Linda Savage

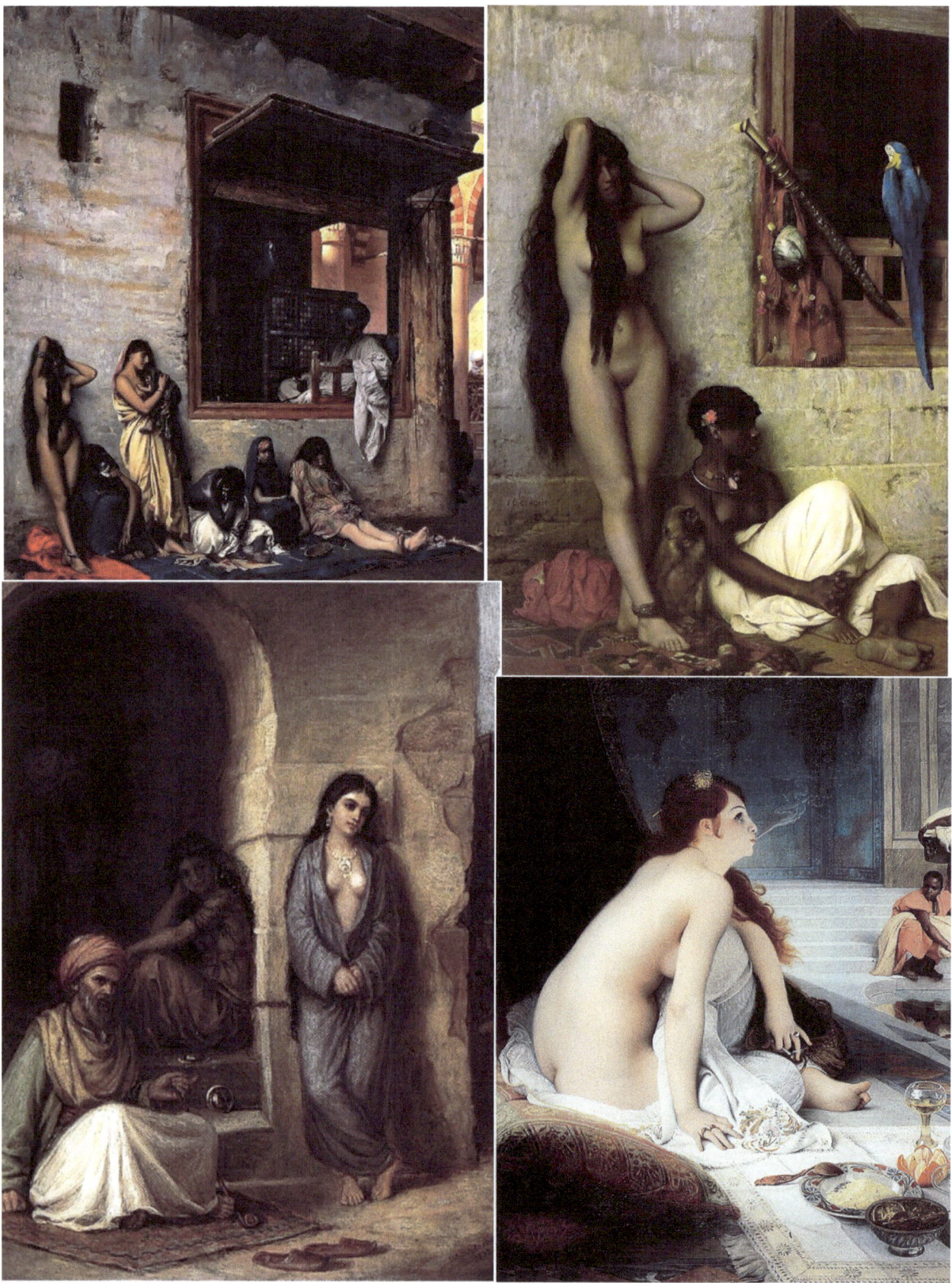

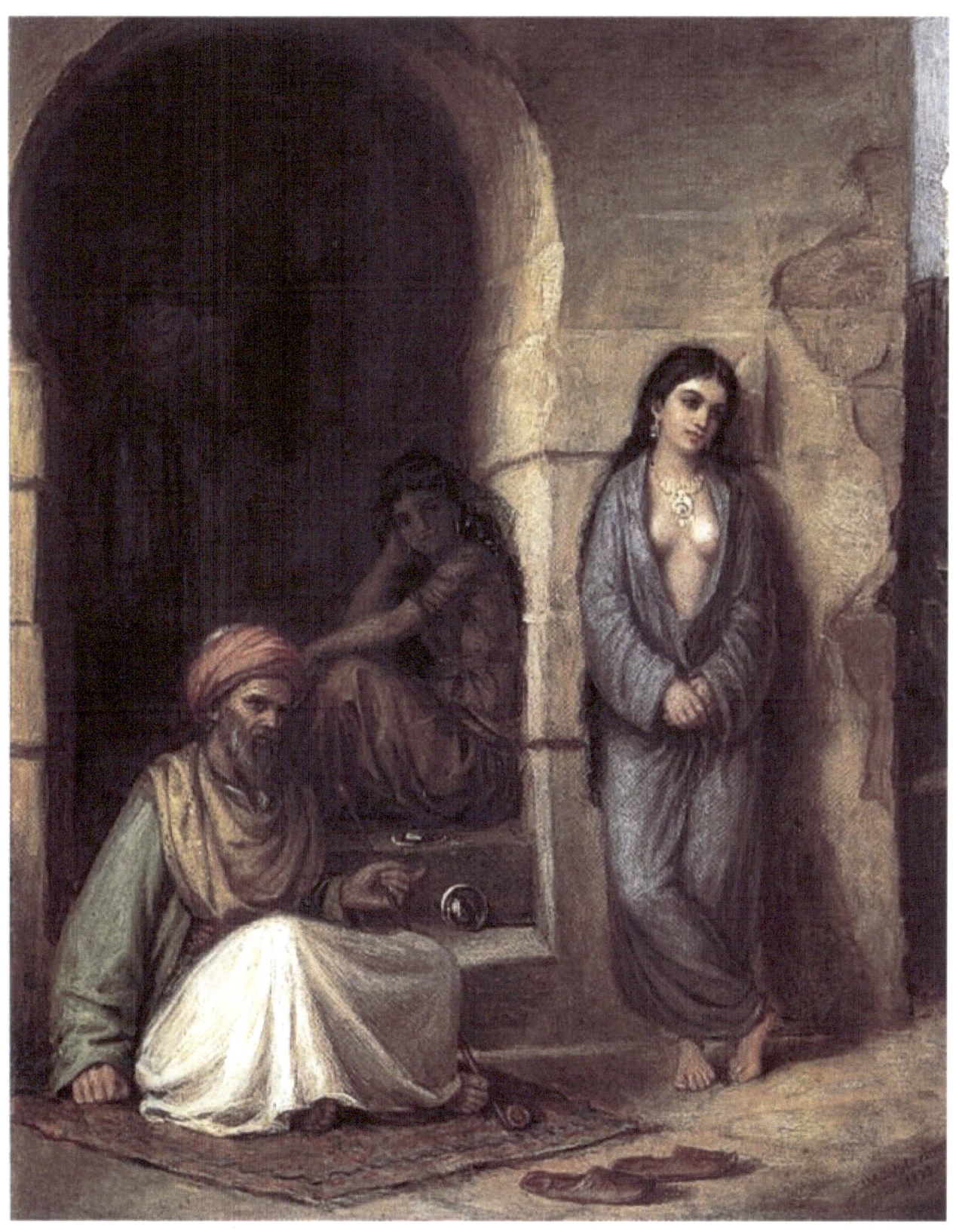

The Slave--John William Waterhouse—1872--Romanticism

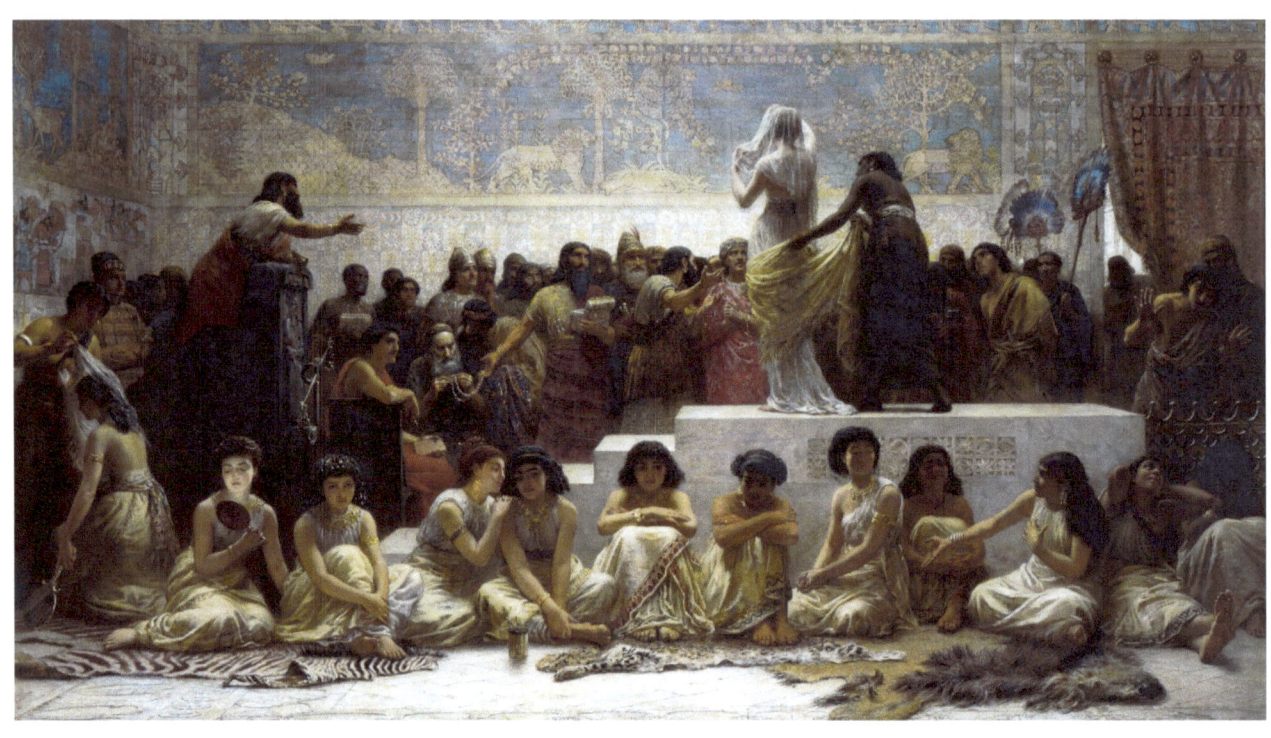

The Babylonian Slave Market (1875) [sometimes called The Babylonian Marriage Market]--Edwin Longsden Long

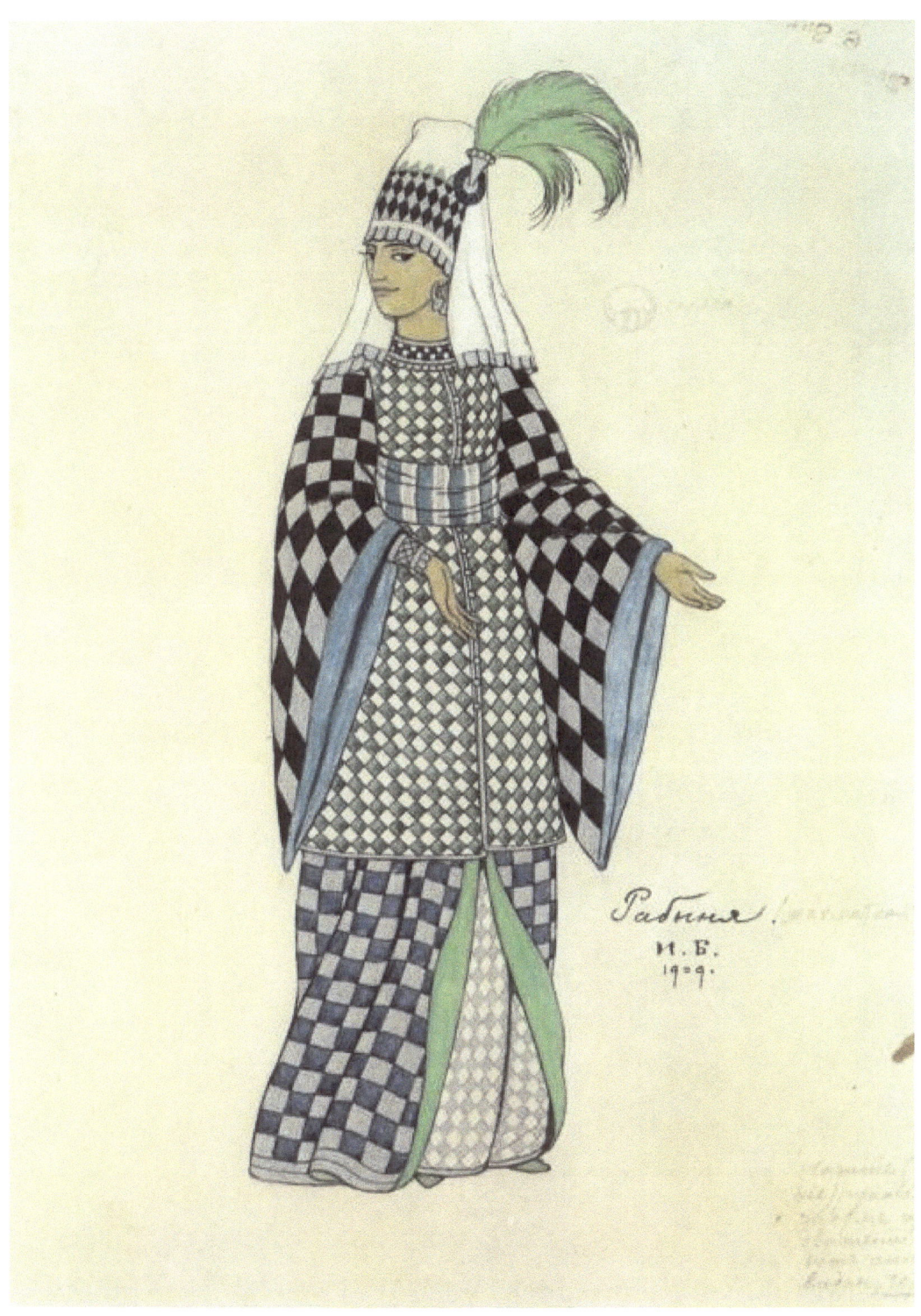

Costume design for the Opera, The Golden Cockerel, by Nikolai Rimsky-Korsakov --Ivan Bilibin—1909--Art Nouveau (Modern)--The Tale of the Golden Cockerel Series

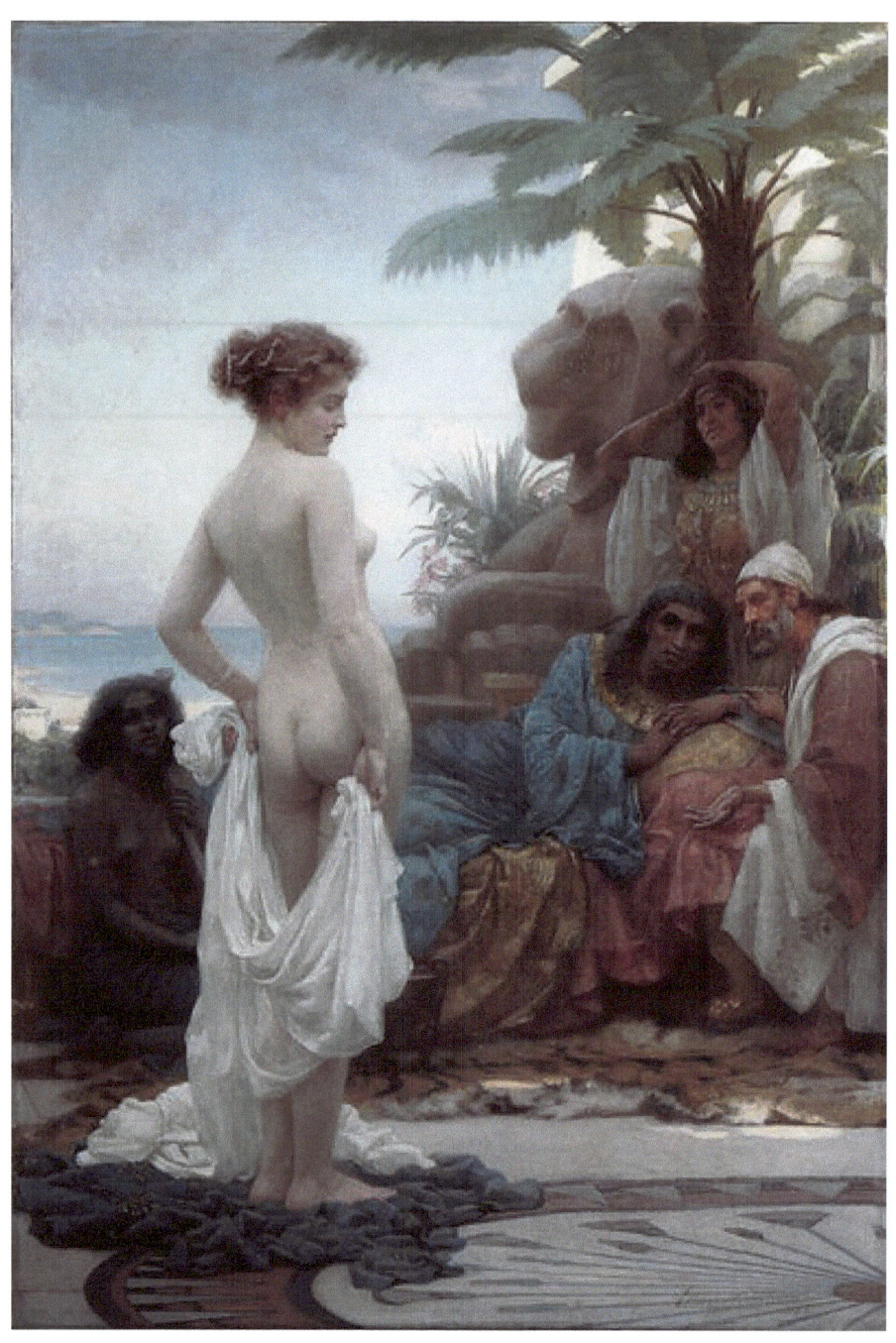

The white slave—1894--Ernest Normand (1859–1923)

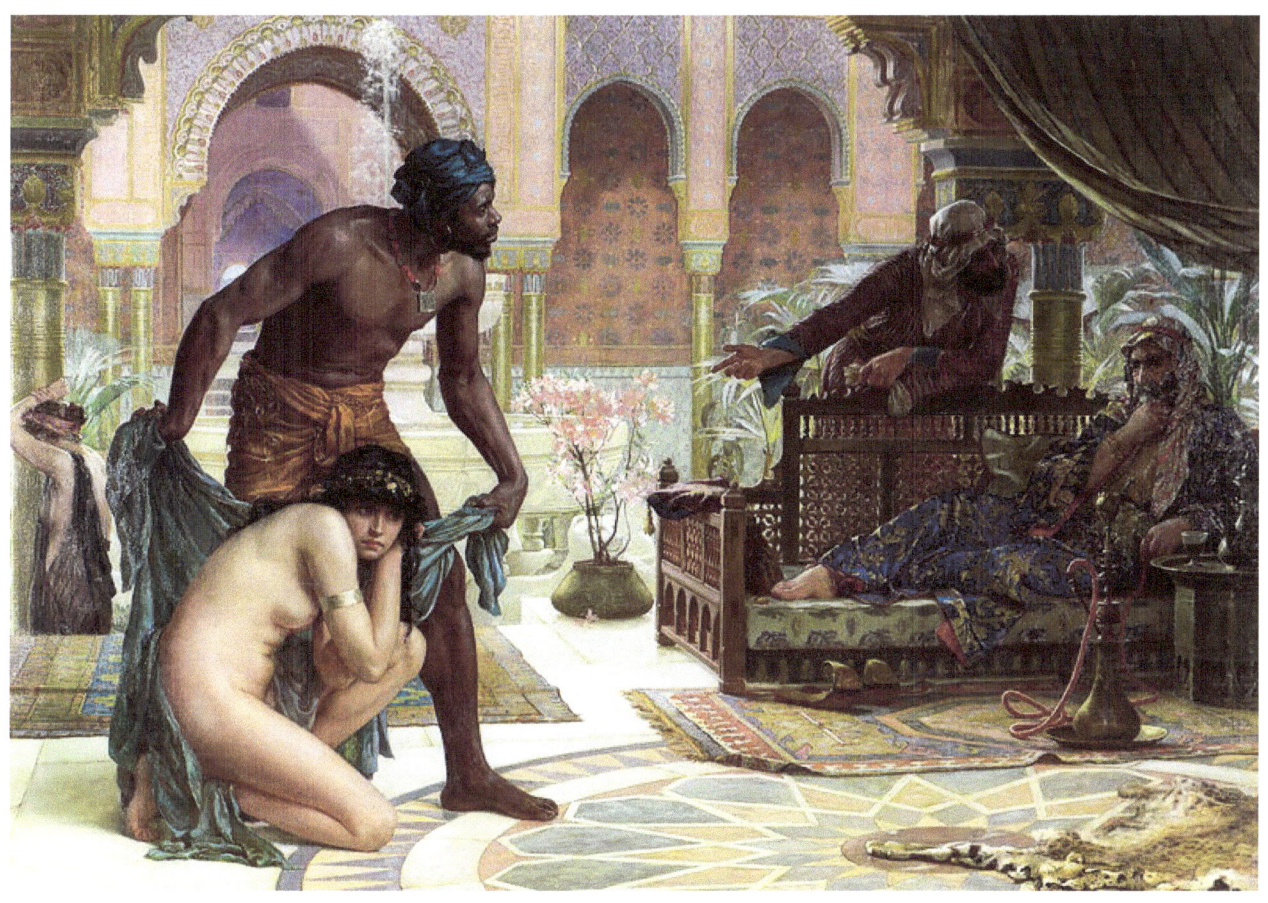

The Bitter Draught of Slavery—1885--Ernest Normand

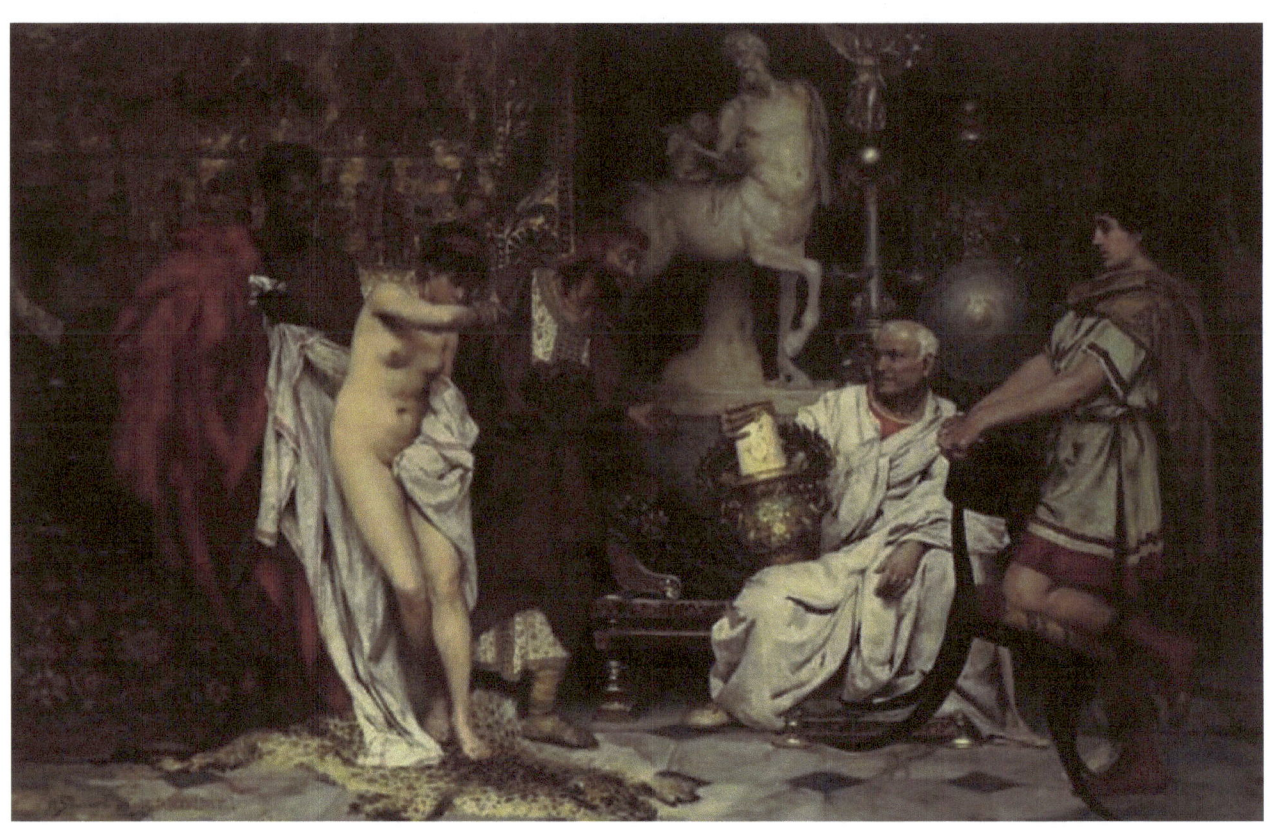

The Girl or the Vase--Henryk Siemiradzki--Academicism

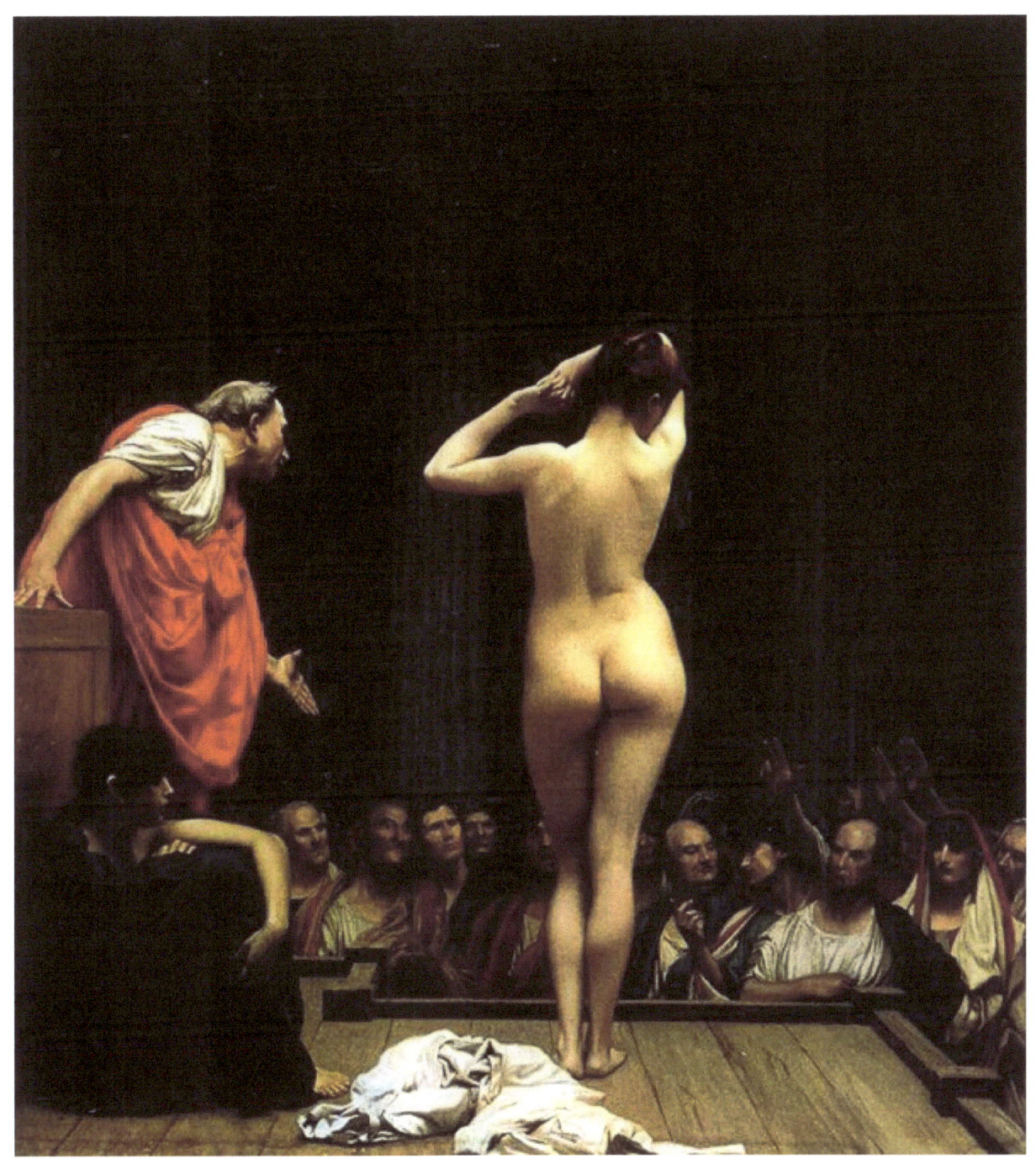

A Roman Slave Market -- Jean-Leon Gerome--Academicism

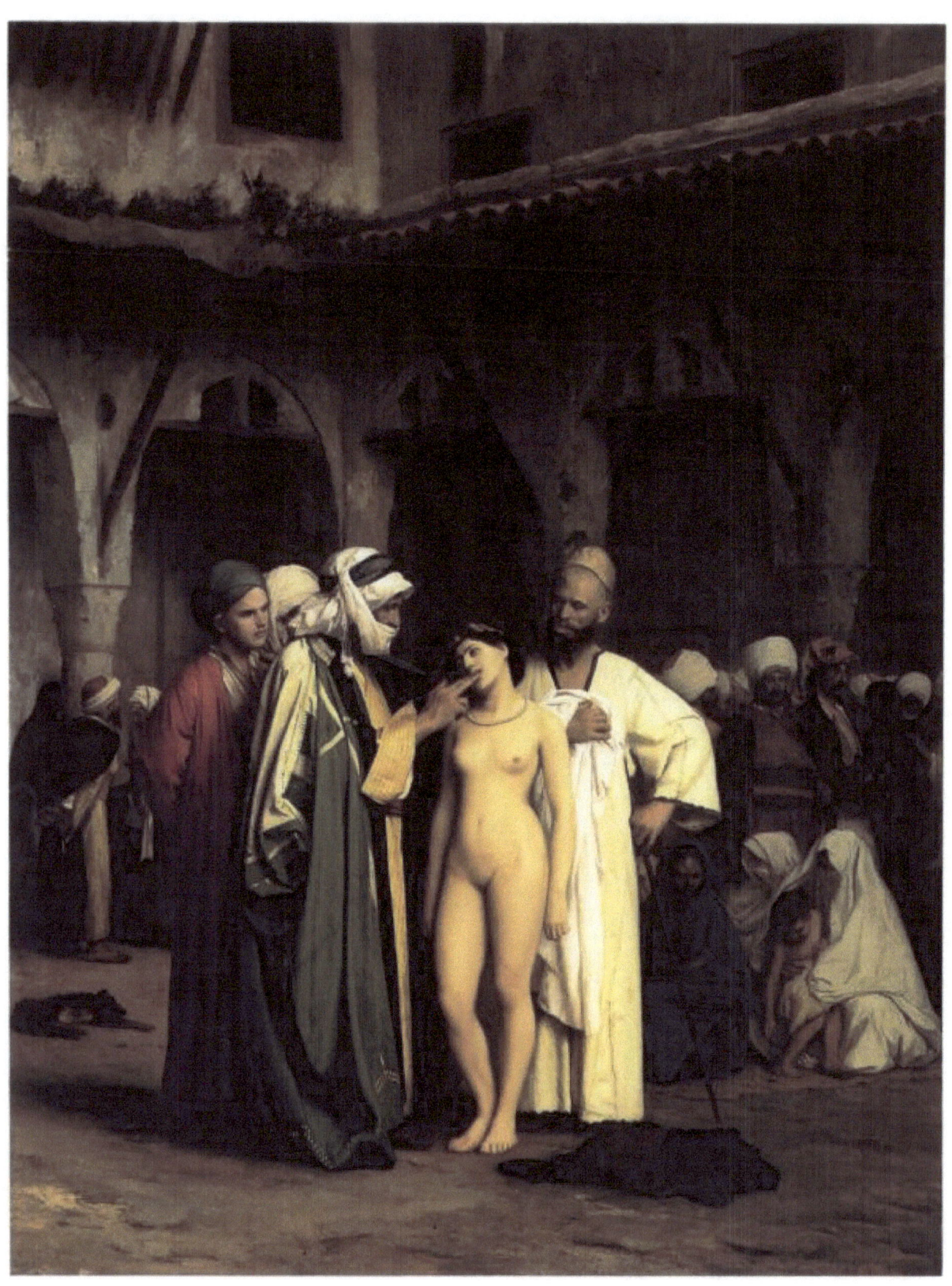

Slave Market--Jean-Leon Gerome—1866--Academicism

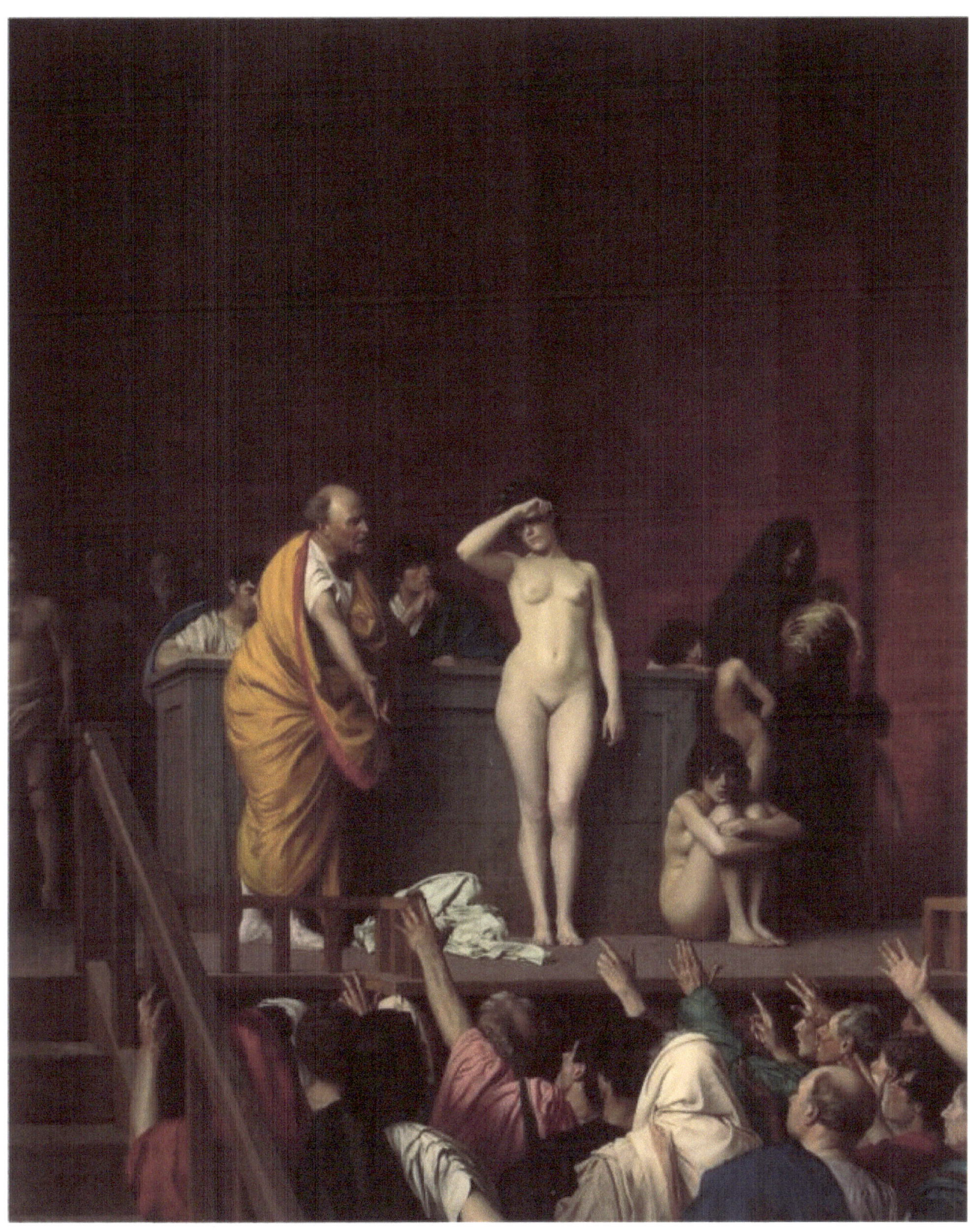

Slave Market in Rome--Jean-Leon Gerome—1884--Academicism

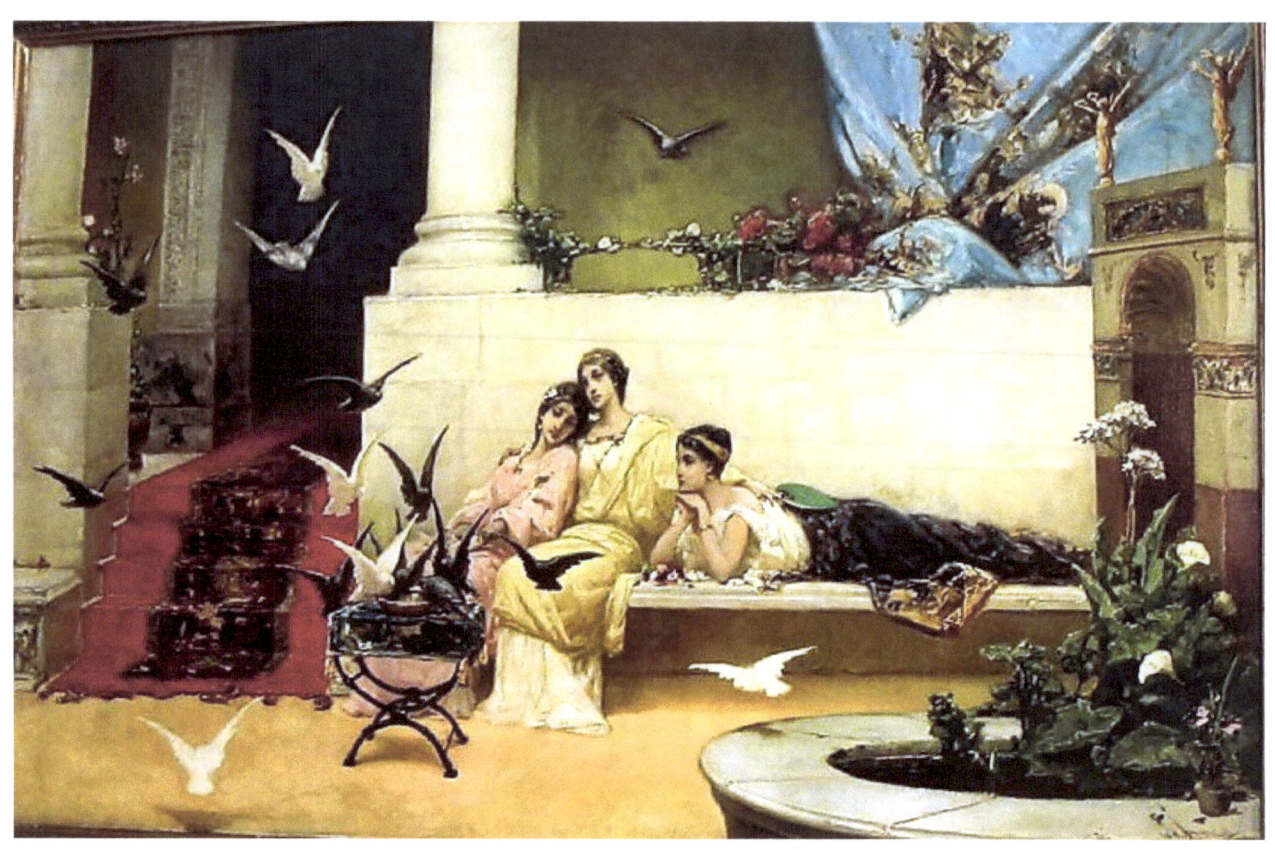

Song of the Slaves--Wilhelm Kotarbinski--Art Nouveau (Modern)

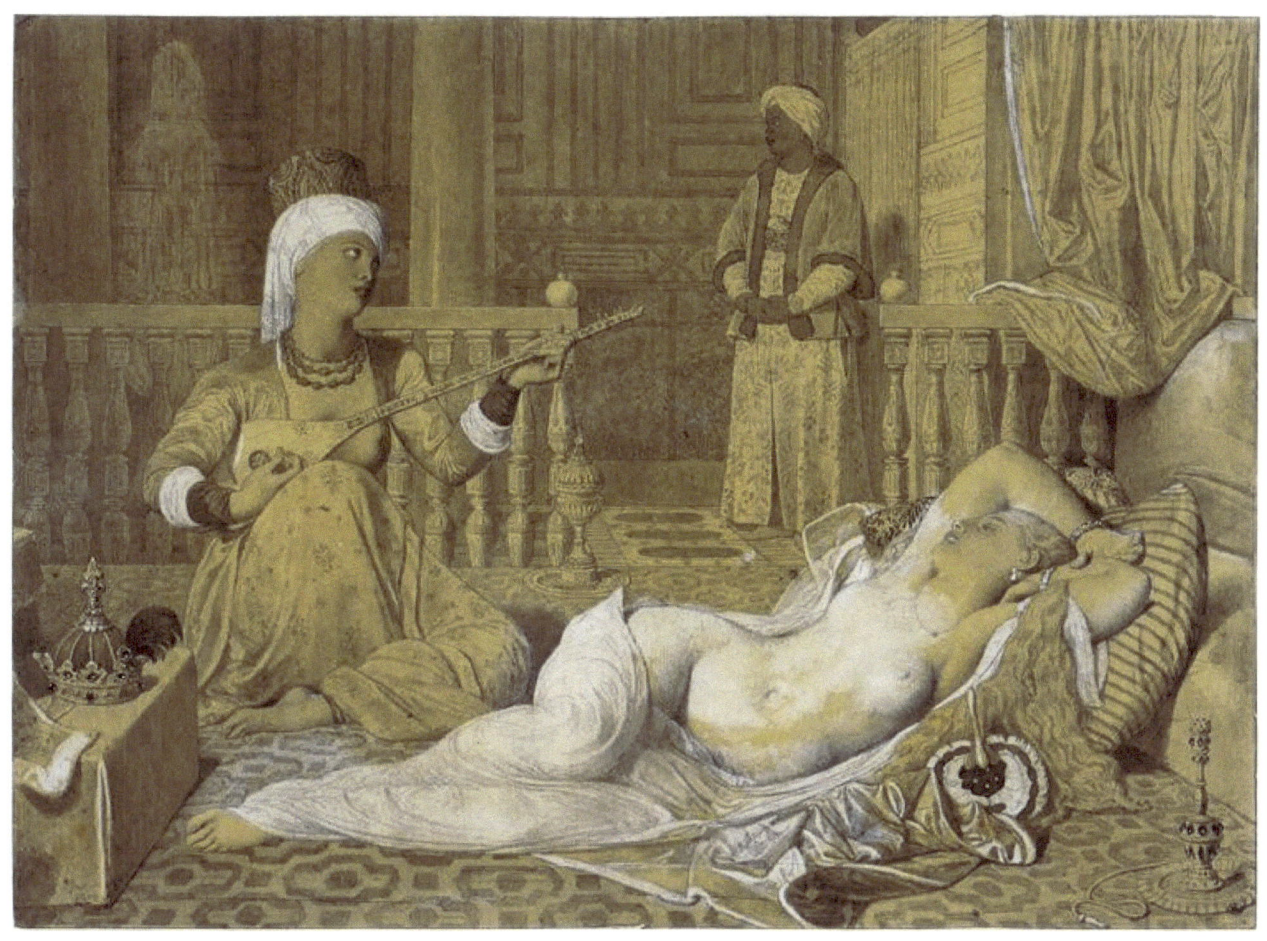

Odalisque with Slave--Jean Auguste Dominique Ingres—1858--Neoclassicism

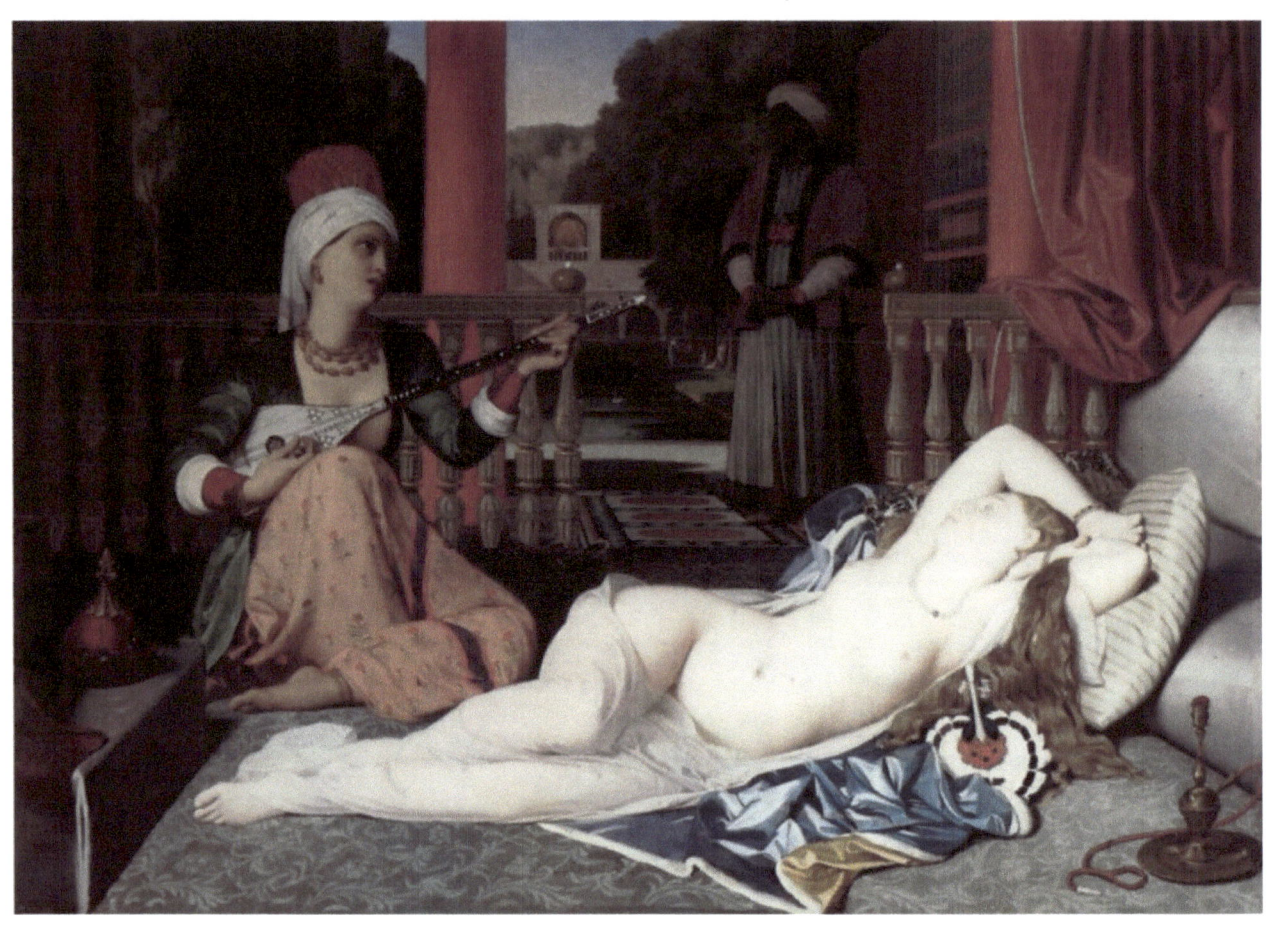

Odalisque with Slave--Jean Auguste Dominique Ingres—1842--Neoclassicism

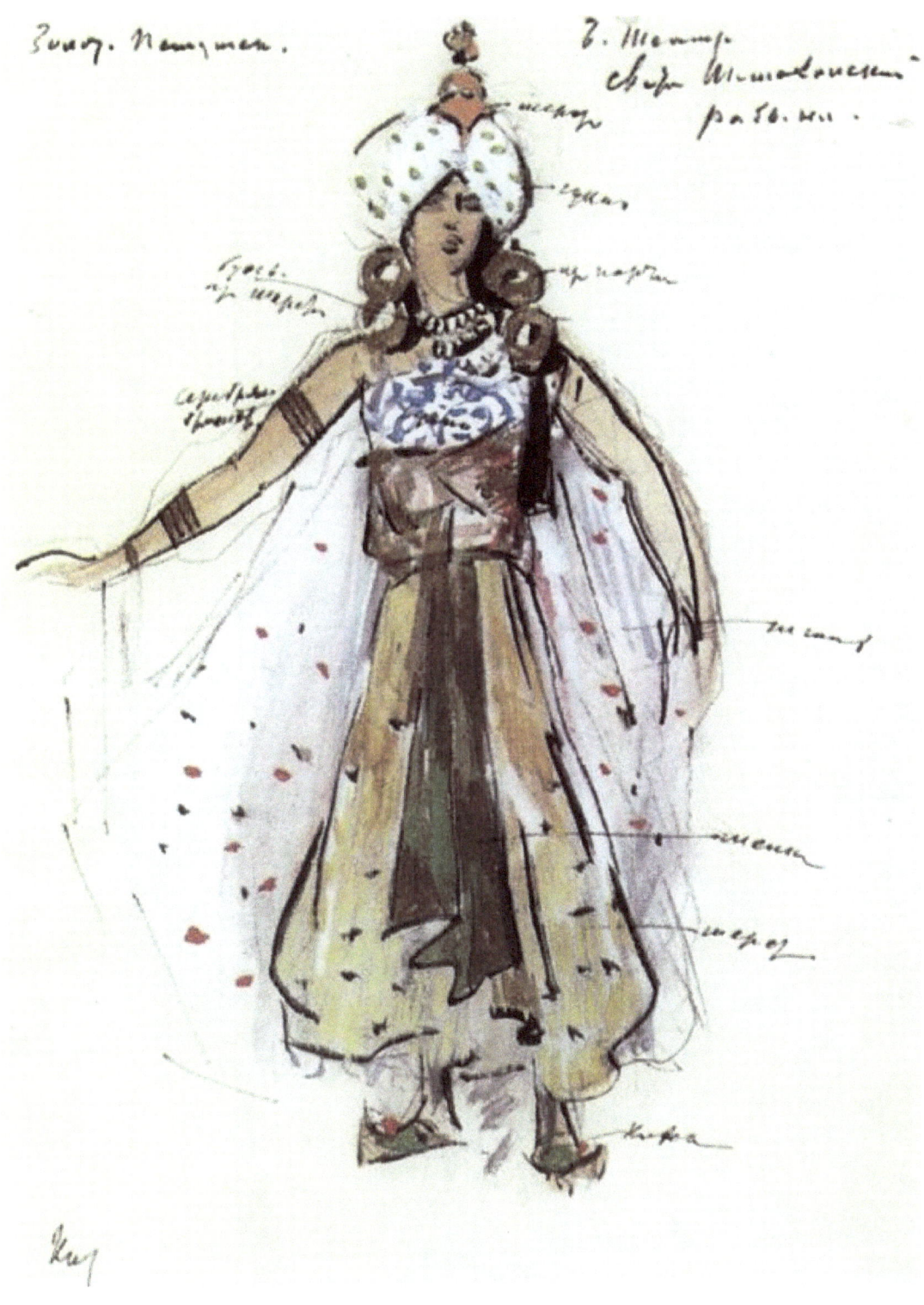

Slave of the queen retinue Shemakhan--Konstantin Korovin—1909--Art Nouveau
(Modern)

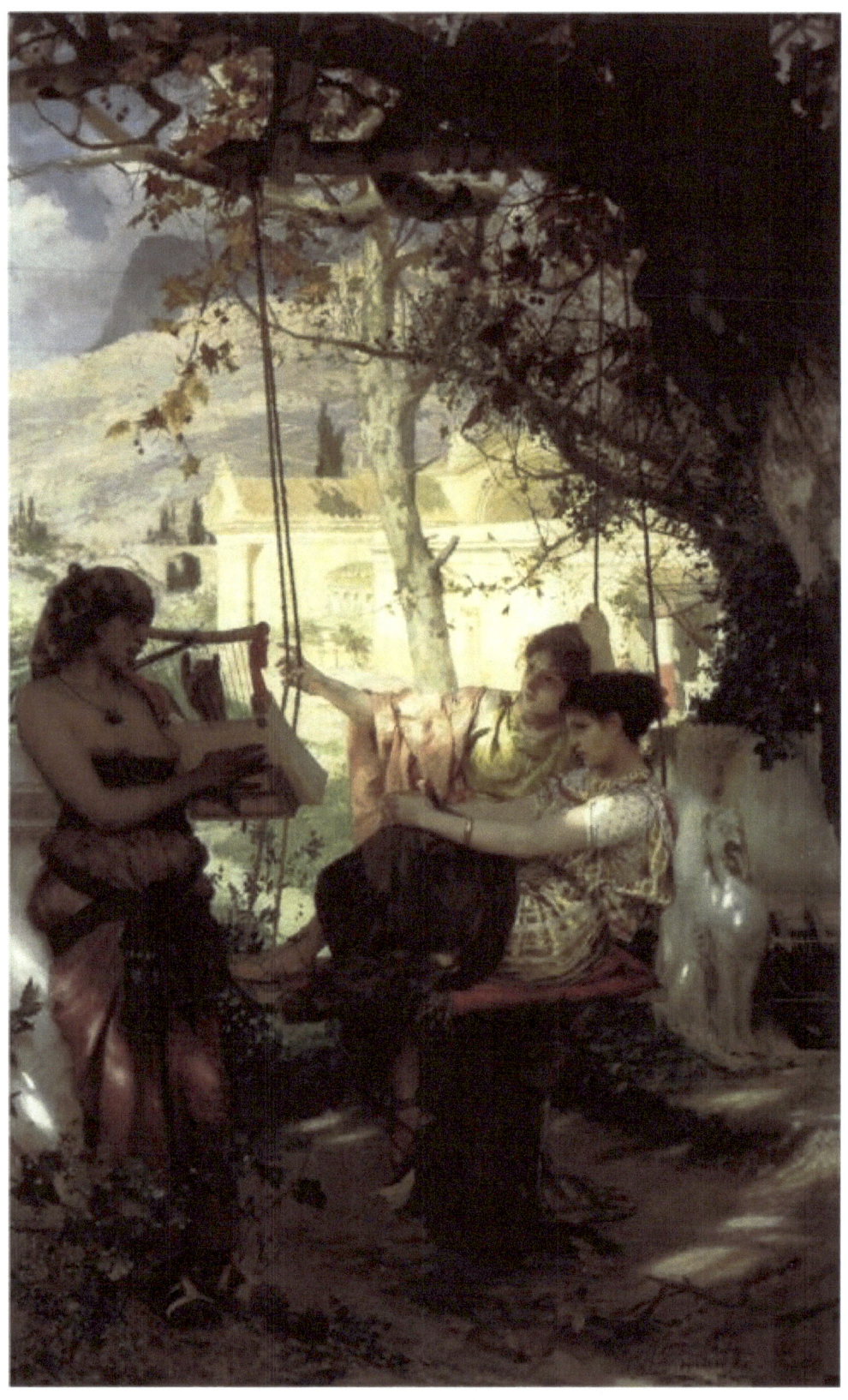

Slave's Song--Henryk Siemiradzki—1884--Academicism

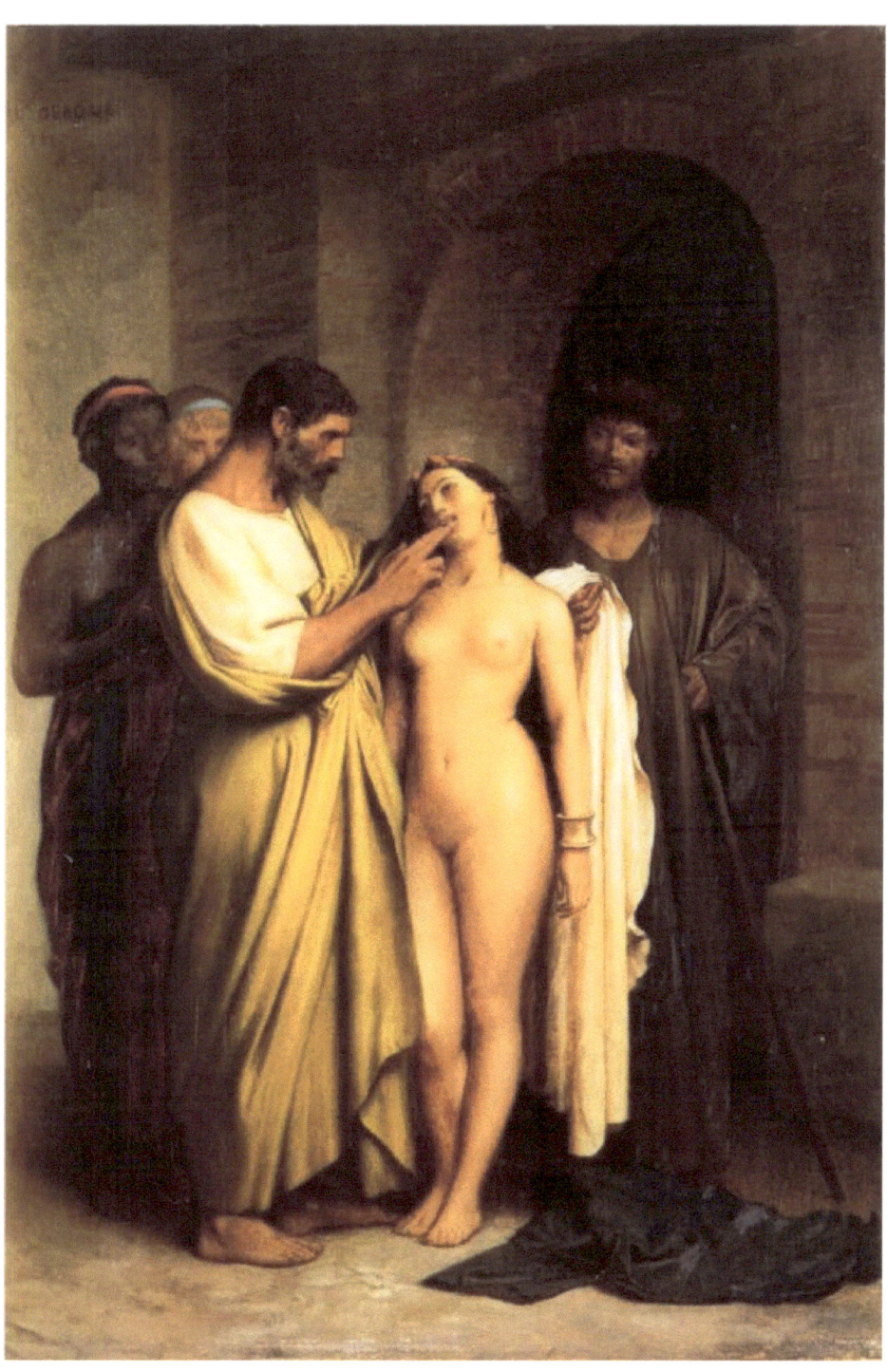

Purchase of a Slave--Jean-Leon Gerome--Academicism

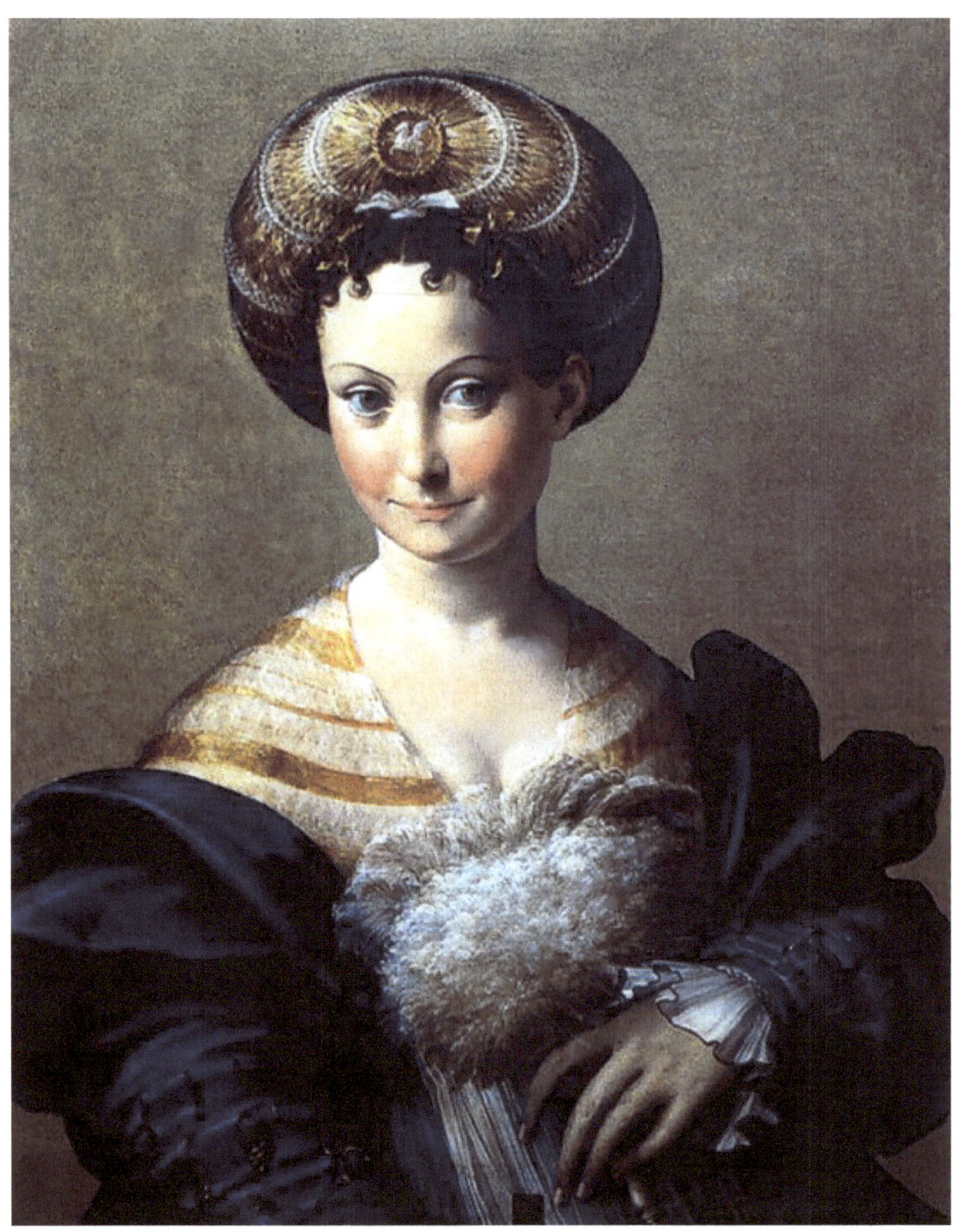

A Turkish Slave--Parmigianino--Mannerism (Late Renaissance)

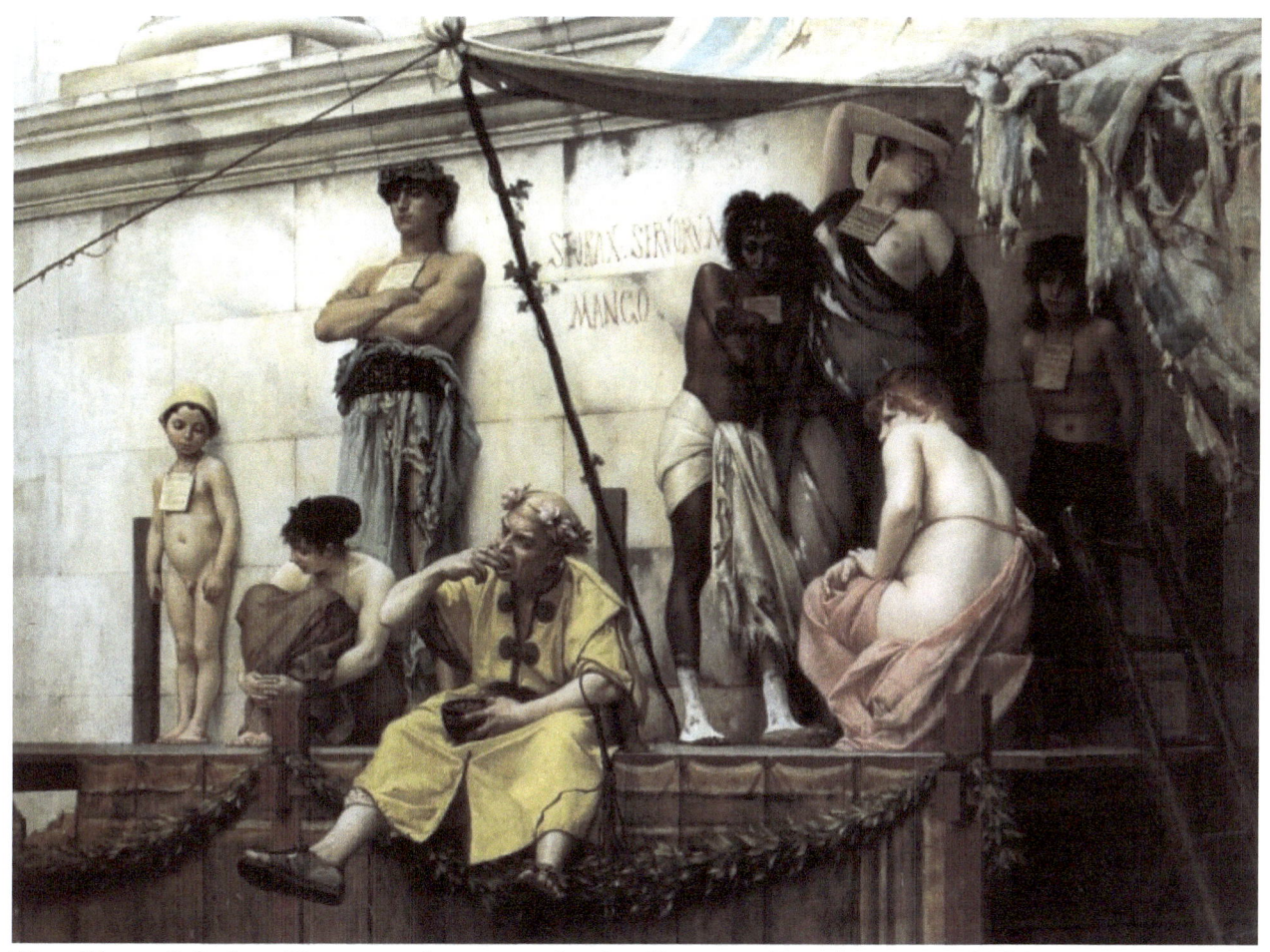

The Slave Market(Roman slave auction)--Gustave Boulanger—1882--
Academicism

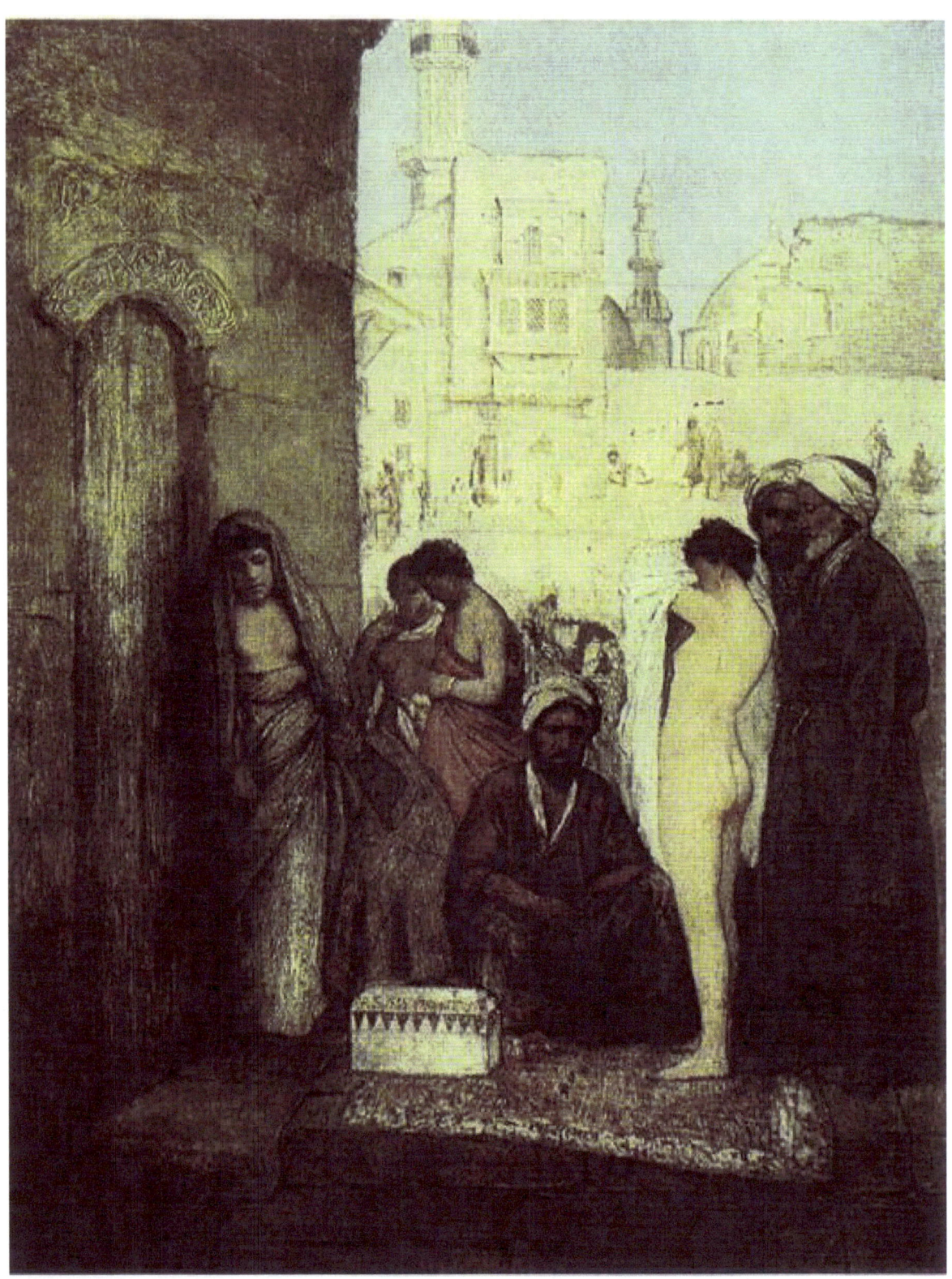

Cairo Slave Market--Maurycy Gottlieb—1877--Realism

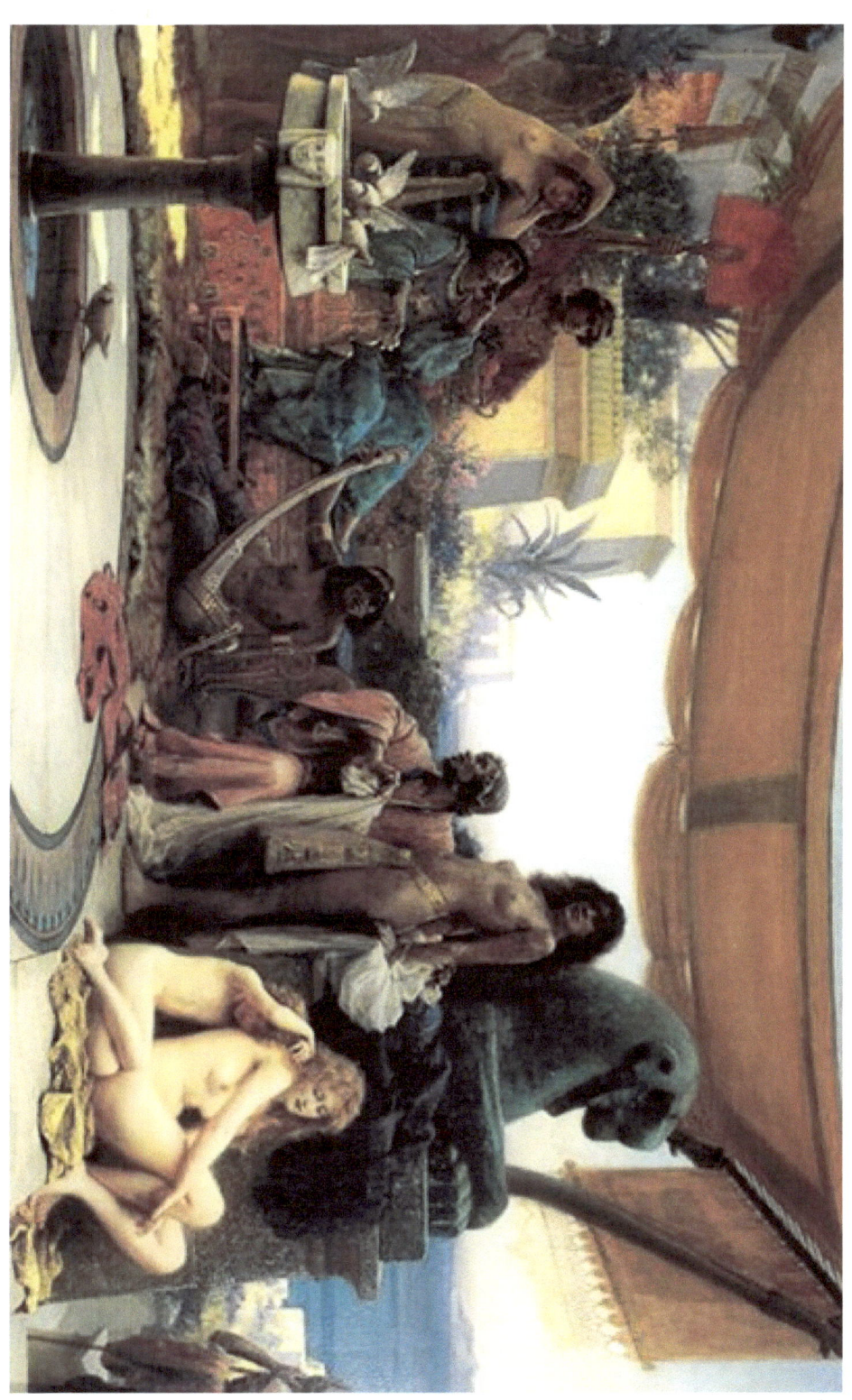

Au Harem—Ernest Norman

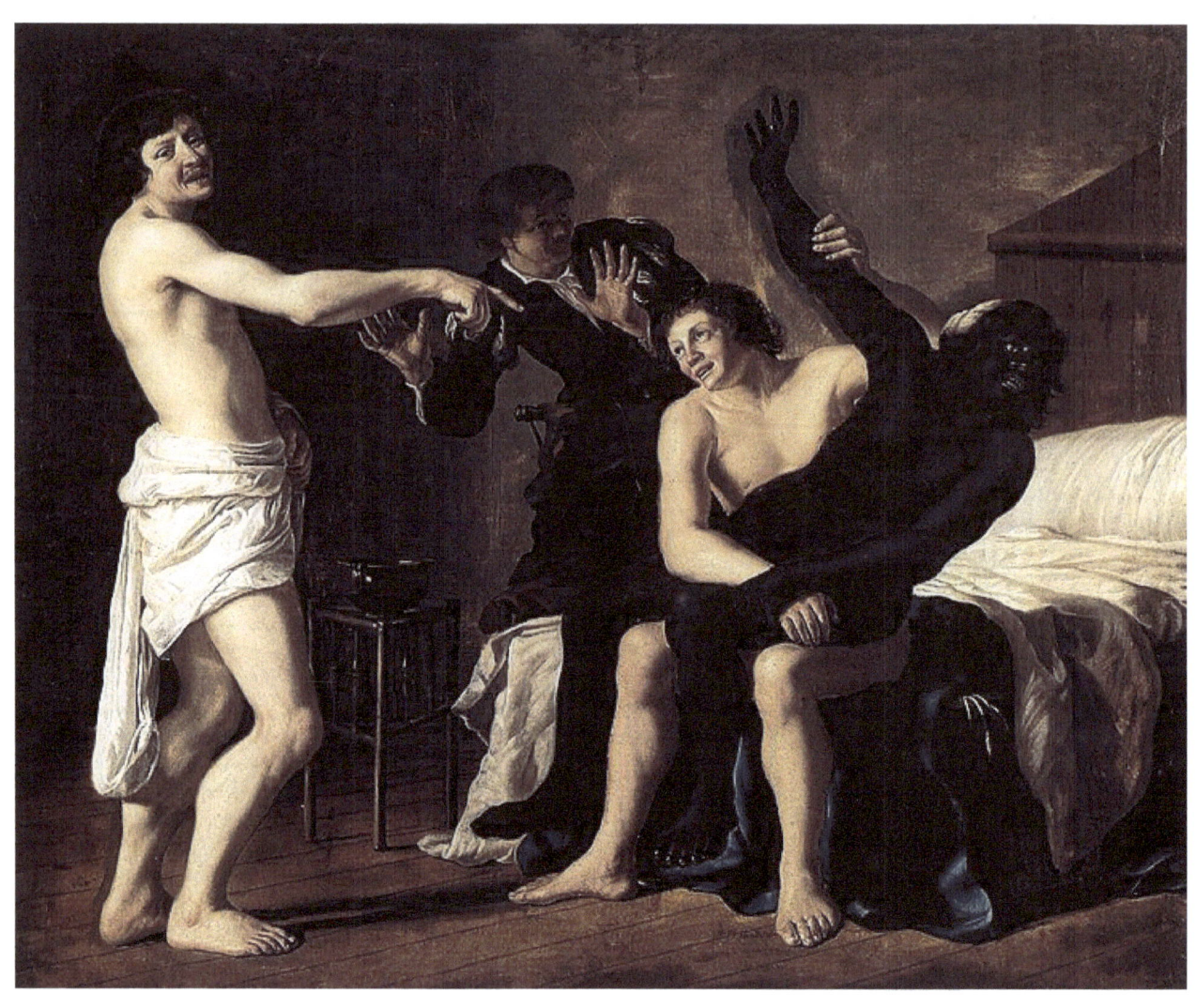

Three Young White Men and a Black Woman--Christiaen van Couwenbergh—

1632

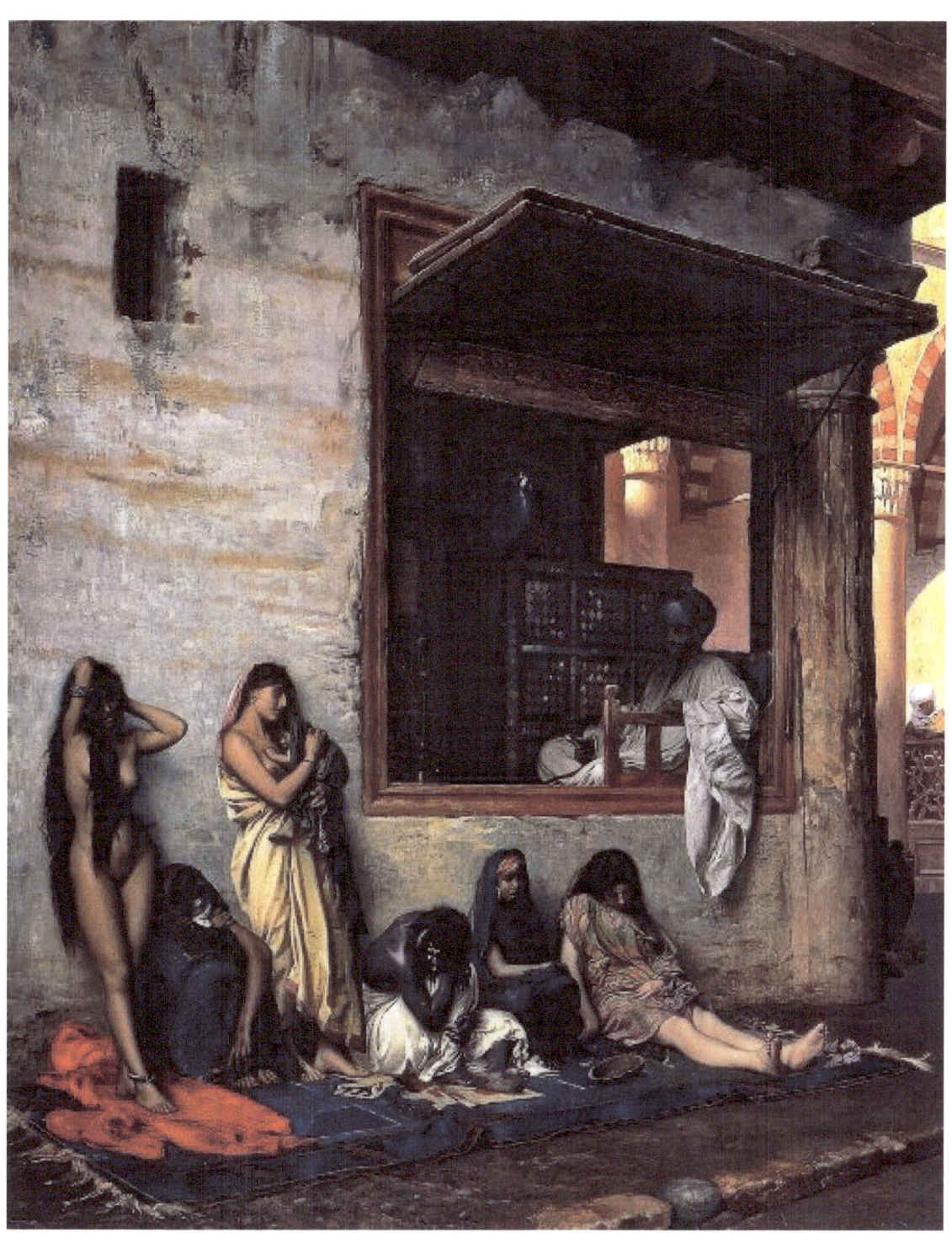

The Slave Market--Jean Leon Gerome

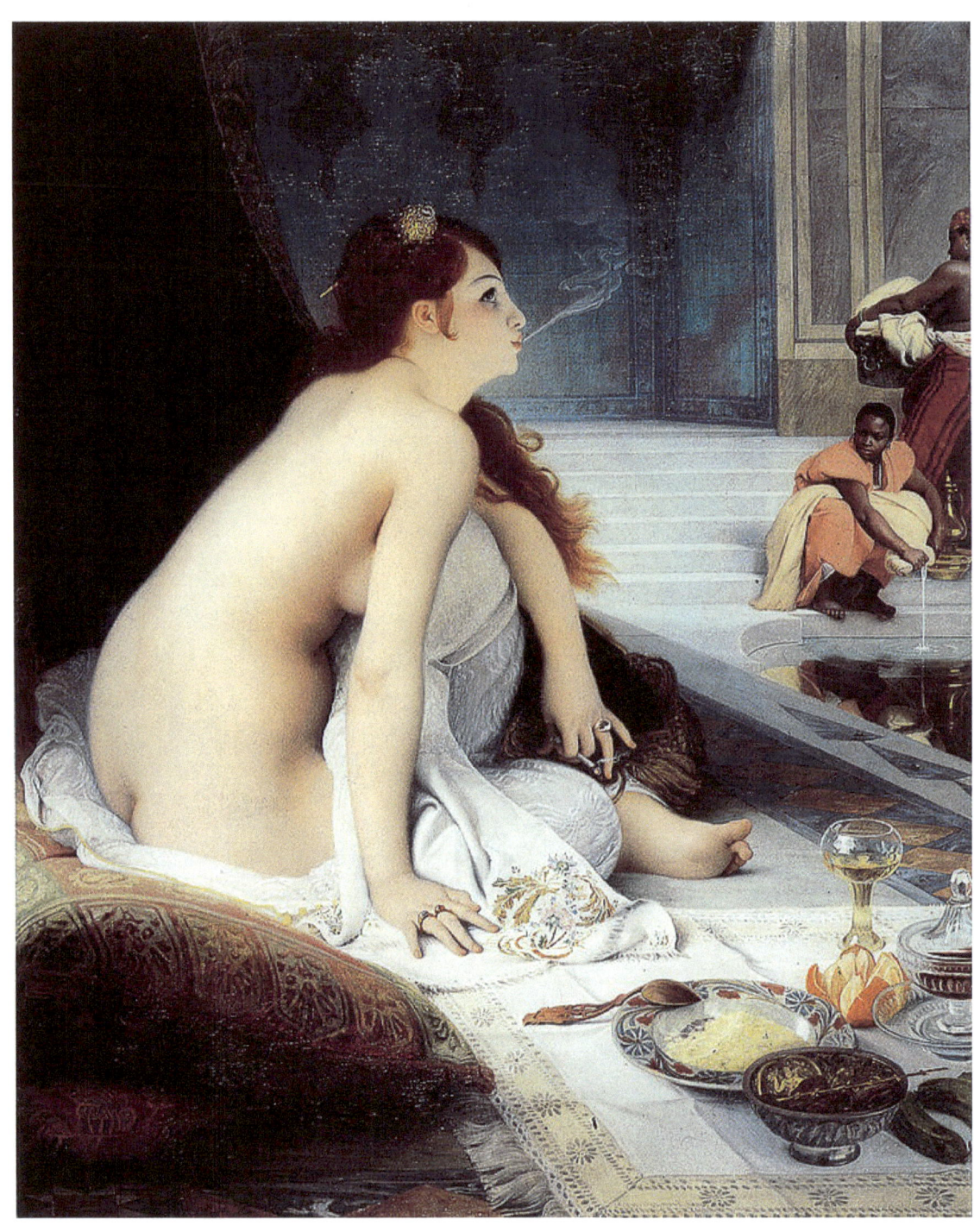

White Slave--Jean-Jules Antoine Lecomte Du Nouy--1888

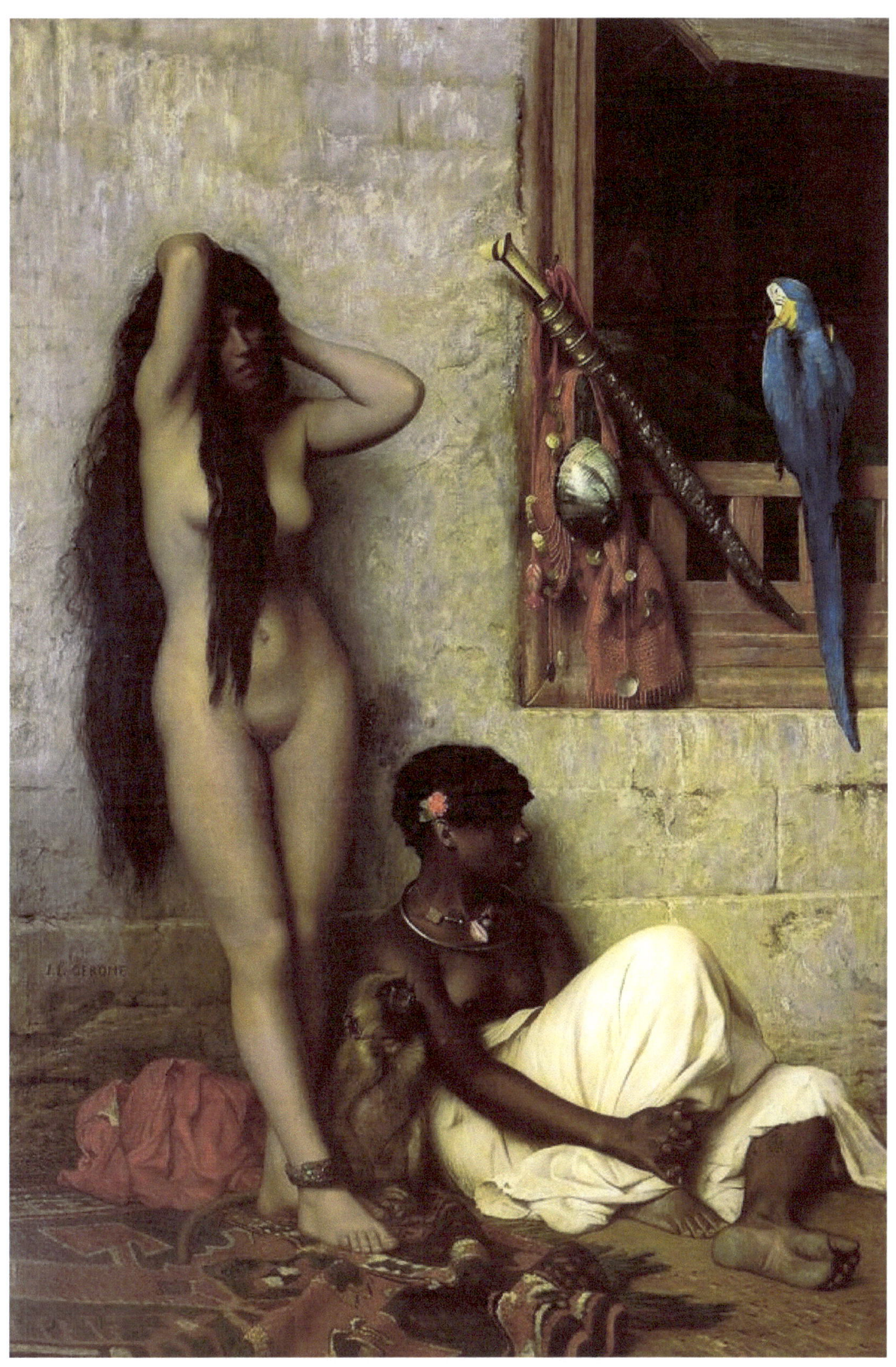

Esclave a vendre--Jean-Leon Gerome

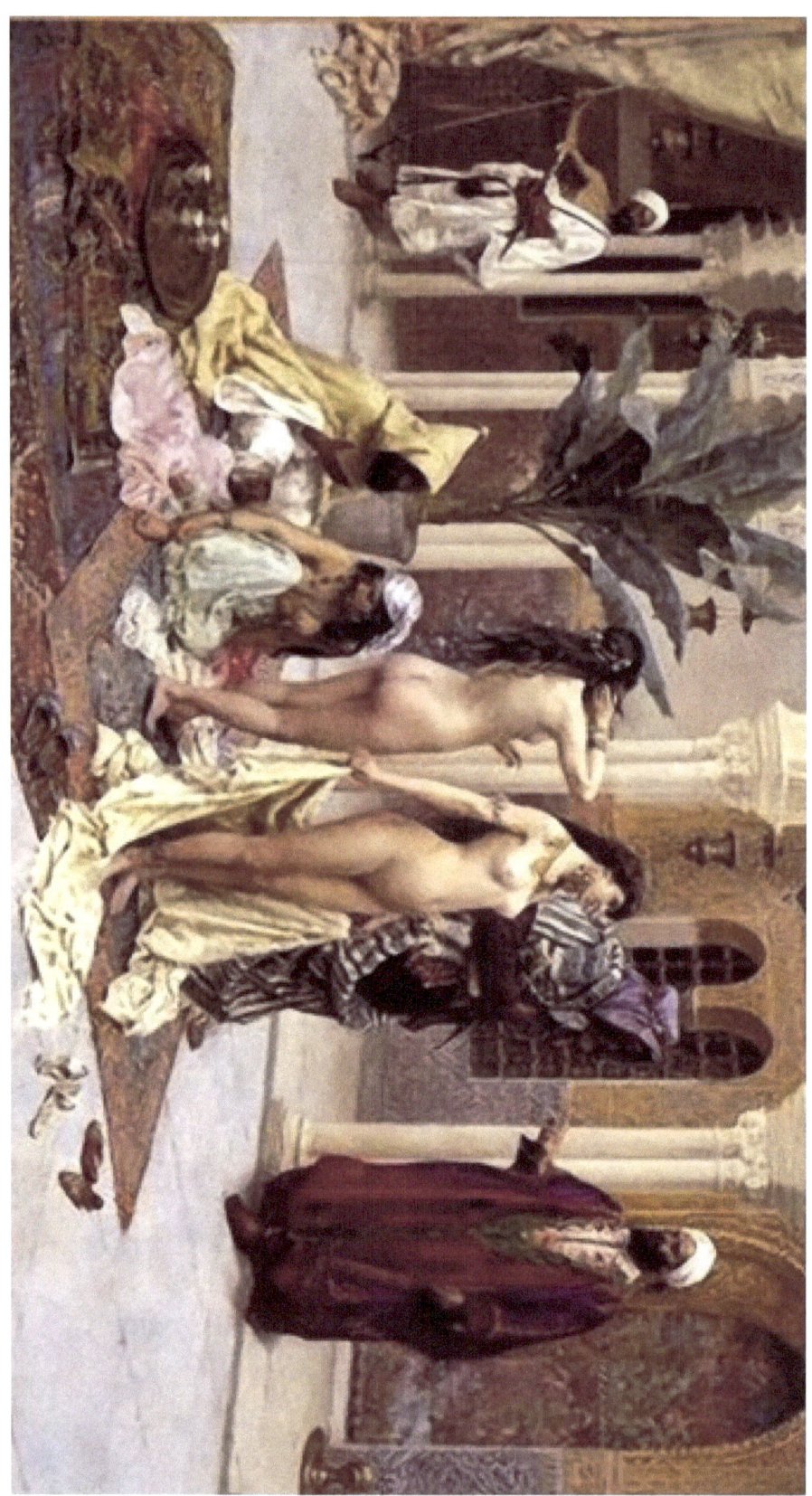

Picking the favorite--Giulio Rosati